D0119560

BRITAIN IN PICTURES

THE BRITISH PEOPLE IN PICTURES

THE HOUSE OF COMMONS

GENERAL EDITOR
W. J. TURNER

The Editor is most grateful to all those who have
so kindly helped in the selection of illustrations
especially to officials of the various public
Museums Libraries and Galleries and
to all others who have generously
allowed pictures and MSS
to be reproduced

THE HOUSE OF COMMONS

MARTIN LINDSAY M.P.

WITH
8 PLATES IN COLOUR
AND
20 ILLUSTRATIONS IN
BLACK & WHITE

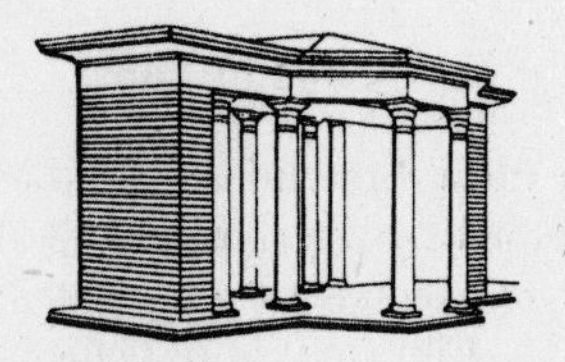

COLLINS · 14 ST. JAMES'S PLACE · LONDON
MCMXLVII

PRODUCED BY
ADPRINT LIMITED LONDON

PRINTED IN GREAT BRITAIN BY
CLARKE & SHERWELL LTD NORTHAMPTON
ON MELLOTEX BOOK PAPER MADE BY
TULLIS RUSSELL & CO LTD MARKINCH SCOTLAND

LIST OF ILLUSTRATIONS

PLATES IN COLOUR

BLACK AND WHITE ILLUSTRATIONS

The New Houses of Parliament designed by Charles Barry
Coloured lithograph by T. Picken after E. Walker, 1852

A DAY IN 'THE HOUSE'

THE Englishman has long been proud of his liberties. Freedom of speech and worship, freedom to choose his own rulers, freedom from arbitrary arrest and all the other despotic impulses of tyrants have been our birthright for centuries. Nor did we need the example of continental nations who surrendered their liberty to dictators, to confirm the advantages of our own way of life. The experience of countless generations of Englishmen lay behind the historic definition of the "four freedoms" drawn up by President Roosevelt and Mr. Churchill. To make these benefits available in less fortunate countries was proclaimed to be our war aim. No such prescription was necessary for the two nations whom the President and the Prime Minister represented. For no Atlantic Charter is needed by the descendants of those who had themselves known Magna Carta.

In England it is the House of Commons that is the guardian of the people's liberties, which twenty generations of Commons men have helped to consolidate. Let us take a look at it at work on any day that Parliament is sitting.

Soon after 2 p.m. the Central Hall begins to fill up ; this is a lobby which anyone is at liberty to enter. Just before half-past, the policemen on duty shout : "Hats off, strangers ! Mr. Speaker !" and then bare their heads. Down the lane through the crowd passes the procession, led by a liveried attendant who precedes the Serjeant-at-Arms carrying shoulder-high the silver-gilt Mace that symbolises the Commons' authority. Immediately behind him is the majestic figure of Mr. Speaker in long grey wig and black silk gown, followed by his train-bearer, chaplain and secretary. The Speaker enters the Chamber and bows to the Commons three times before taking his place in front of his Chair. That he now looks round at the Members and then prays for the Country is perhaps the oldest joke in connection with Parliament. But at this stage the Speaker's Chaplain does indeed say prayers, and amongst them sometimes that of Speaker Yelverton (1597-1601) "to expel darkness and vanity from our minds and partiality from our speeches."

Meanwhile, the lobby adjoining the Chamber has been filling up with other Members, who crowd round the window of the Vote Office to collect the pale blue Order Paper which is the agenda for the day. As soon as Prayers are over they enter the Chamber, those belonging to the Government party seating themselves to the right of the Speaker and those of the Opposition to his left. Ministers and Government Whips on the one side, and ex-Ministers and others of prominence belonging to the Opposition facing them, sit in the front row. In front of Mr. Speaker's raised Chair, these two benches, though opposite each other, are separated by the great table upon which rests the Mace, and at which sit the three be-wigged Clerks who record the proceedings. At the far end is a seat for the Serjeant-at-Arms, who still wears the sword which was the symbol of his authority to carry out Mr. Speaker's orders in more turbulent times. Here and there a woman Member is seated and perhaps provides a colourful contrast to the sober, sub-fusc suits of the males.

On four days of the week the proceedings usually open with Questions which occupy the first hour. Mr. Speaker calls the Member in whose name the first Question stands. He rises and says : "Number One, Sir." The appropriate Minister then gets up from the Treasury Bench and reads out the reply which has been prepared by his Department. The Question may deal with any of the many subjects within his responsibility. For example, "to ask the Minister of Pensions under what circumstances an ex-Serviceman in receipt of a disability pension can obtain an increase on marriage." The Minister's reply is to the effect that such a man will be eligible for an increased pension if his marriage takes place within ten years of his war service. Immediately a dozen Members rise to ask a supplementary question, and the Speaker calls one or two alternately from each side of the House before passing to Question No. 2. A Member will now ask the Minister if he does not consider the ten-year limit very harsh. To this the Minister

By courtesy of the Provost and Fellows of King's College, Cambridge

KING HENRY VI WITH REPRESENTATIVES OF THE LORDS AND COMMONS
Detail from an illuminated charter of 1445-1446

By courtesy of the Lord Great Chamberlain

A SEVENTEENTH-CENTURY SPEAKER

Sir Edward Turnour, Speaker, 1661-1672

Oil painting by John M. Wright

will reply that he "cannot accept the Hon. Member's imputation" ; or that the present regulation is more generous than that of previous Governments; or (sometimes) that he will reconsider the matter, in which case the Member who framed the Question has achieved his objective.

If a new Member has been elected at a by-election, he takes his place immediately after Questions. He marches up the aisle—known as "the floor of the House"—between two sponsors, bows, takes the oath and shakes hands with the Speaker, all to the cheers of his supporters and the counter-cheers of the party opposite, and perhaps a proud smile from a fond wife seated in one of the galleries above.

Mr. Speaker then directs : "The Clerk will now proceed to read the Orders of the Day." The Clerk rises and announces : "National Service Bill : Second Reading"—or whatever it may be. Thereupon the responsible Minister goes to the table, puts his notes on the despatch box, and speaks for between one and two hours upon the alleged merits of his Bill. Once or twice he may be interrupted by "Before the Rt. Hon. Gentleman leaves that point, will he kindly explain . . ." but it is not often that he is stopped, if only because those most interested in the measure are probably anxious to speak themselves. The Minister's speech is followed by one from the Opposition Front Bench, at the end of which at least a score of Members rise, hoping to "catch the Speaker's eye." Mr. Speaker calls whoever he considers will contribute most usefully to the Debate, but traditionally he will give priority to anyone wishing to make a maiden speech. For this occasion the Member starts with the diffident and time-honoured request that the House will show him indulgence. After this modest beginning he sets about his subject with usually no perceptible lack of self-confidence. But whatever the quality of his contribution, the Member who follows offers him the congratulations of the House which, he is assured, has seldom listened to a more promising maiden speech.

The speeches continue, hour after hour, for the House does not adjourn for meals. But once every few weeks the Debate is suddenly interrupted by Black Rod, who arrives to summon the "faithful Commons" to the bar of the House of Lords to hear the Royal Assent given to previous Bills. Black Rod invariably finds the Commons' door locked in his face, and he is not admitted until he has knocked three times. As we shall see in due course there were once excellent reasons for this procedure, as also for the fact that when the moment comes to make financial provision for the Minister's Bill, or for any other Money Resolution, the Speaker leaves the Chamber, his place being taken by another Member presiding from a seat at the table.

The House usually thins out about 5 p.m., to fill up again soon after eight. The Debate stops at 10 p.m., unless the House has decided to suspend this rule as on occasions of exceptional importance or controversy (or unless business of certain special "exempted" classes is on the agenda), when it may be much later. The last half-hour is always available to a private Member who has successfully balloted for the opportunity to bring up a subject of his own choosing, often the individual case of one of his constituents. At 10.30 p.m. the great light above Big Ben is switched off and the House adjourns to the immemorial call of: "Who goes Home?" Sleepy Members of Parliament tuck their brief-cases under their arms and stroll through Westminster Hall, which in eight and a half centuries has known the tread of every sovereign and every leader of the nation. And so out into New Palace Yard—"new" since 1098—hoping that the last tube has not gone.

A wise bishop once wrote: "the roots of the present lie deep in the past." Let us turn back the pages of the history books and delve into the past, in order to see how we have got here.

THE CRYPT: THE HOUSE OF COMMONS
One of the carved bosses of the painted wooden roof, *c.* 1327

THE GREAT SEAL OF THE COMMONWEALTH, 1651

HISTORICAL RETROSPECT

THAT part of London which is known to us to-day as Westminster was at one time an island in the Thames : a low-lying, stinking mud-flat covered by dense thickets, known as "The Island of Thorns" and referred to as a "terrible place" in early Saxon chronicles.

It is first mentioned in connection with an obscure religious fraternity, for whom the seclusion of this forlorn locality had a special attraction. In the seventh century, or thereabouts, they built a group of monastic dwellings on the island, to which was added a royal residence by King Canute, 1017-1035 ; tradition says that this was the scene of the famous incident of his ordering back the tide.

Canute's successor, Edward the Confessor, frail in constitution and monkish in character, decided to build a permanent religious centre upon this spot already consecrated by generations of holy men. The new abbey was from the first known as West-Minster, being built to the west of the other minster already standing at St. Paul's. In order more easily to superintend the work, the King built himself a home opposite. This is the origin of the Palace of Westminster, and of the famous Abbey which was consecrated in 1065.

A year later William the Norman invaded from Caen in Calvados (in reverse of the procedure of 878 years later), and in due course was crowned in the Abbey. He enlarged the palace of the Confessor and it is recorded that he held Councils there—the first meetings of a form of Parliament at Westminster.

But the Councils of the Conqueror were not the first held by kings of England. There had already been the Witenagemot, an assembly of the most trusted counsellors summoned when the monarch felt in need of advice. For kings had learnt that it was inadvisable to make laws without prior consultation with those who would be affected. Accordingly they had long been accustomed to hold "deep speech" with the Witan, in different parts of the kingdom, two or three times a year. And, like the House of Commons to-day, the ancient Witan was, to some extent at least, an assembly of territorial representatives.

It was the Conqueror's red-haired son who conceived the magnificent idea of Westminster Hall, which still stands to-day in many ways unique among the great halls of the world. Certainly no other building has seen so much pageantry, or is so rich in English history. William II used it to dispense justice in, and as a banqueting chamber. Through the north doorway, which now admits black-hatted M.P.s, carrying umbrellas and brief-cases, once rode the King's Champion between the tables of the roystering nobles to challenge any that disputed the Sovereign's right to rule. The vent to give exit to the smoke from the roasting oxen is still to be seen in the roof—that roof which has looked down both upon steel-clad barons despatching one of their number to the scaffold and, more recently, steel-helmeted legislators mounting tubular scaffolding to despatch incendiaries. Even the fine carved beams and arches are in accordance with English history. They were originally made of Rufus's Norman chestnut, to be replaced by Sussex oak when the alien monarchy had taken root in English soil. And when, some twenty years ago, the ravages of the death-watch beetle necessitated their replacement, it was discovered that the best English oak was to be found on the same estate, still belonging to the same Sussex family, as it had originally come from six hundred years earlier!

So, down the centuries, Westminster Hall has been the scene not only of the barbaric pageantry of feasting and court festivities, but also of many activities through which has gradually developed the pattern of British life. Successive kings used it as an audience chamber, as a senate house for the earlier meetings of Parliament, and as a Palace of Justice. In it took place most of the great state trials, from that of Sir William Wallace in

THE KING'S CHALLENGER ENTERING WESTMINSTER HALL
Engraving by M. Yeates, 1684

1305 to those of the Jacobite lords of '15 and '45, and later that of Warren Hastings which lasted for no less than seven years.

The last great ceremonial occasion on which it was used was when King George V lay in state in 1936, and nearly a million of his sorrowing people filed silently past.

From William Rufus onwards, each king made additions or improvements to the Palace, which was their principal residence. To Stephen, 1135-1154, is attributed the chapel named after his patron saint. Later, as we shall see, St. Stephen's was diverted from its sacred purpose to house the Commons, and it was in this medieval chapel that most of the historic parliamentary battles took place. But in 1512 a fire destroyed much of the Palace, causing Henry VIII to move out, and since that time the King has never lived at Westminster. Parliament was accustomed to meet in the Palace because, when the King sent for his advisers, it was convenient to call them to his own residence.

The earliest of these assemblies consisted of the King's chief officers of state, and of the great feudal and spiritual lords, the earls, barons, archbishops, bishops and abbots; they were summoned by name by the King, who in person presided over their councils. But in 1254 each county sheriff was bidden to send two knights to Parliament. This established a precedent of great constitutional importance. Firstly because these representatives were to be chosen, not by the Crown, but by those whom they were to represent, and secondly because they were summoned "*to consider what aid they would give to the King in his great necessity.*" Thus began the power to grant or withhold supplies, the lever which was subsequently used time and again by the representatives of the people in their efforts to control the activities of the King and his executive. And it is this power of the House of Commons to withhold the revenue without which no government can govern for any length of time, which is still to this day our greatest safeguard against tyranny. The origin of modern parliaments was perhaps the Council summoned by Simon de Montfort in 1265; for in this, for the first time,

THE TRIAL OF THE EARL OF STRAFFORD IN WESTMINSTER HALL, 1641
Etching by Wenceslaus Hollar

THE CORONATION DINNER OF JAMES II IN WESTMINSTER HALL
Engraving by S. Moore, 1685

there were not only knights from the shires but also citizens and burgesses representing and elected by the new cities and boroughs.

So the great prelates, nobles, knights and burgesses began to meet fairly regularly in Parliament, either in Westminster Hall or in some other convenient chamber in or near the Palace (though occasionally they met elsewhere than in London : for example, in Oxford, York, Northampton and once in Coventry). Gradually they tended to divide on social grounds, and thus in the course of time grew up the two components of the legislature: the Lords and the Commons. This separation dates from the fourteenth century. The name "Commons" signified originally the "communes" or organised communities from which the representatives came, but modern emphasis is upon the common people who are represented.

For two hundred years—from about 1350 to 1547—the Chapter House of Westminster Abbey was the usual meeting place of the Commons, owing, no doubt, to the difficulty of finding accommodation in the Palace for their increasing numbers. Through all this period the responsibilities of the Commons were growing and the power of the people consolidating. For instance it was Edward I who gave the royal assent to the Statute of Tallage, which provided "that no tallage or aid shall be taken without the assent of the archbishops, earls, knights, *burgesses and other freemen of the land.*" In the reign of Edward III, 1327-1377, we find that the Commons had passed the stage of being merely advisers on taxation, and were already legislating for the regulation of trade. But as yet no more. For they shrank from advising the Crown upon so difficult a subject as state policy. When asked their opinion about peace with France, they replied: "Most dreaded lord, as to your war and the equipment necessary for it, we are so ignorant and simple that we know not how to devise." Soon, however, pressure of events, the consequence of the King's incompetence, was to sweep away their diffidence.

One by one, concessions necessary to safeguard the people were wrested by the Commons from reluctant monarchs. So Henry IV, in 1407, acknowledged that grants of supply must originate in the Commons (less susceptible than the Lords to manipulation by the Sovereign), and from the reign of Henry VIII legislation ceased to be by Petition, being forever after by Statute. Hitherto, it had been found that the King's legislation often fell a good deal short of a Commons' petition. From now on whatever measure was required was presented to the King in the form of a Bill which he could only assent to *in toto*, or face the row if he chose to dissent.

After Henry VIII's death the Commons began to meet in St. Stephen's Chapel, which they were to do until the great fire of 1834, almost three hundred years later. To this we owe an important constitutional development. The seating in this narrow, rectangular chapel could only be conveniently arranged on two sides facing an aisle down the centre, which gave great encouragement to the inception of two mutually antagonistic parties sitting opposite each other. The logical development of this was of course the conception of Government and Opposition, with the latter's duties of constructive criticism and the provision of an alternative government, which in itself provides the most powerful safeguard against maladministration with its logical consequence of revolution.

It is impossible to overestimate the effect upon our history of that casual decision. For had the Commons been allotted a square room, they would almost certainly have sat, as in foreign chambers, upon semi-circular benches. This would have encouraged numerous groups of opinion shading from left to right, and would probably have resulted in a continuous series of weak administrations always at the mercy of some new majority alignment.

From the time that the Commons moved across from the Abbey Chapter House to St. Stephen's, documentary records of their proceedings become increasingly available. In the reigns of Mary and Elizabeth they seem to have concerned themselves chiefly with match-making on their sovereigns' behalf. In neither case were these efforts greatly appreciated. Mary's reply

By courtesy of the Corporation of London

VIEW SHOWING WESTMINSTER BRIDGE, THE PALACE AND ABBEY

Oil painting. School of Samuel Scott, c. 1751

By courtesy of the Trustees of the British Museum

NEW PALACE YARD AND ENTRANCE TO WESTMINSTER HALL

Water colour by T. Coney, 1807

was: "We have heard much from you of the incommodities which may attend our marriage to Philip of Spain, but we have not heard of the commodity which is of some weight with us—namely our private inclination." So the wedding took place and twelve months later the King and Queen held a court in Westminster Hall, of which it is recorded:

"The Queen sat highest, richly apparelled and with her Belly laid out, that all men might see she was with Childe. . . . Notwithstanding the Queen's display, and that public thanksgivings were made on the occasion, it appears that her supposed pregnancy arose from dropsical affections."

Queen Elizabeth's reply to the Commons' representation was: "I intend to spend my own life for the good of my people . . . Children are uncertain blessings and for myself it would be enough that a marble stone should declare that I reigned such a time, lived and died a virgin." But, when importuned with further matrimonial advice a few years later, she tartly observed that the Commons "had small experience and acted like boys."

On occasions Elizabeth treated the people's representatives with no little contempt. It was she who was responsible for the first recorded cases of Members of Parliament being imprisoned for speeches that found disfavour with the Crown. Nevertheless, Elizabeth's Parliamentarians founded the system of poor-law administration and steadily developed the sphere of domestic government.

In 1605, two years after James I's accession, occurred the famous Gunpowder Plot. The Catholics, who had been reduced to despair by the severity of Queen Elizabeth, were disappointed in their hopes of redress under King James. So a few hot-headed spirits, including Guy Fawkes, tunnelled under Parliament Square and filled one of the Lords' cellars with twenty barrels of powder. The plot was discovered when one of the conspirators sent warning to a peer, who was advised to absent himself from Parliament on account of a great yet hidden danger to which he would otherwise be exposed. In due course "Guido Fawkes was drawen, hanged and quartered in the Old Palace Yard at Westminster," and every year thereafter a detachment of the Yeomen of the Guard in scarlet and gold, carrying lanterns and pikes, has searched the cellars before the Opening of Parliament.

The quarrels between the Crown and the Commons gathered momentum during the reign of James I, but it was in those of his son and grandson, Charles I and II, that the great struggle for constitutional liberty was to be resolved, though not until much blood had been shed.

Maddened by the Commons' insistence upon their privileges, James sent for them and tore up all their Bills before their eyes. Then he committed a Member to the Tower, asserting his right "to punish any man's misdemeanours in Parliament, as well during their sitting as after." The Commons' reaction was to enter a protest in their records, affirming that "the liberties of Parliament are the ancient and undoubted birthright and inheritance of the subjects of England and . . . every Member of the House hath, and of good right ought to have, freedom of speech . . . and freedom from all impeachment, imprisonment and molestation other than by censure of the House itself." The King's anger knew no bounds. He mutilated the offending Journal, dispersed the authors of this resolution in various prisons and the House itself by adjournment.

It was the vindictive characters of monarchs which dictated certain precautionary procedure in the Commons which is still by custom followed to-day. Thus Members concealed identities by referring to each other not by their names but by those of their constituencies, which presumably afforded some protection before official lists were published. And the Speaker was always moved out of the Chamber by resolution, and his place taken by a Member, whenever supplies were to be discussed, so that he should not be in a position to give information to the King as to which Members were being obstructive.

Charles I had been on the throne barely twelve months before he was involved in a furious quarrel with the Commons over the fate of two Members whom he had imprisoned. This was the first of many disputes, in all of which the King was to come off second best.

Repeated attempts to raise taxation without the authority of Parliament resulted in the Petition of Right, which set out that "no man hereafter be compelled to make or yield any gift, loan, benevolence, tax or such-like charge without common consent by Act of Parliament." Charles was forced to accept this declaration, but soon began to evade its provisions. After dissolving Parliament, which was not to meet again for eleven years, he proceeded to levy illegal dues in the form of poundage and tonnage.

But when, after this long interval, lack of revenue obliged the King to convene Parliament again, those determined men immediately sat down to discuss popular grievances, taking up matters where they had been dropped eleven years before. The first action of the "Long Parliament" (1640-1653) was to pass a Bill enacting that the interval between Parliaments should never in future exceed three years. This was followed by a declaration of the illegality of the King's recent extortions.

Charles retaliated by attempting to arrest the five Members—Pym, Hampden, Hazlerig, Holles and Strode—who were leading the Commons. They were warned in time and departed down river. Leaving his guard at the door, the King strode into the Chamber and seated himself in the Speaker's Chair. Seeing that none of the Members he sought were present, he demanded their whereabouts of Speaker Lenthall who, on his knees, replied in the classic phrase : "May it please your Majesty, I have neither eyes to see nor tongue to speak in this place, but as this House doth direct me, whose servant I am." No wonder the Sovereign has never since been admitted to the House of Commons, and even the messenger, Black Rod, has to knock three times !

THE EXECUTION OF CHARLES I IN WHITEHALL, 1649
Engraving from a contemporary Dutch news-sheet

Another attempt on the part of the headstrong monarch to arrest the five Members, who had taken refuge in the City of London, having failed, Charles's friends tried to induce him to concede that sovereignty belonged to the King in Parliament and not to the King alone. "Not for an hour," he replied imperiously, and withdrawing to York he began to make preparations for the inevitable civil war.

For five years Cavalier and Roundhead fought for mastery. Meanwhile the Long Parliament, in British fashion, continued to meet to review the progress of the war. And when the Commons found that their troops were being repeatedly beaten by the dash and daring of Prince Rupert's cavalry, they chided Hampden in much the same fashion as their successors did Neville Chamberlain after his reverses just three hundred years later.

The final defeat of the royalist forces in 1648 resulted in the impeachment of the King by the Commons on the charge that "by the fundamental laws of this Kingdom, it is treason in the King of England to levy war against the Parliament." The trial took place in Westminster Hall, and Charles's head was struck off in Whitehall.

Many of the Parliamentary party in the Commons had by this time suffered altogether too much at the hands of the Crown. So it is perhaps not surprising that, within a week of Charles's execution, they passed a resolution to the effect that monarchy was "unnecessary, burdensome and dangerous." The Commons also affirmed that "the House of Peers in Parliament is useless, dangerous and ought to be abolished." Legislative effect was given to these sentiments, but it was by no democratic administration that the sorely-tried nation was now to be governed. For Cromwell forcibly suppressed the Long Parliament when he discovered that it was about to disband his standing army. The speech with which he did so still remains a classic of robust invective :

"It is high Time for Me to put an End to your Sitting in this Place, which you have dishonoured by your Contempt of all Virtue, and defiled by your Practice of every Vice. . . . Is there a single Virtue now remaining amongst you? Is there one Vice you do not possess? Ye have no more Religion than my Horse! Gold is your God: Which of you have not bartered your Conscience for Bribes? Is there a Man amongst you that has the least Care for the Good of the Commonwealth? Ye sordid Prostitutes, Have you not defiled this sacred Place . . by your immoral Principles and wicked Practices? Ye are grown intolerably odious to the whole Nation; You were deputed here to get Grievances redressed; Are not yourselves become the greatest Grievance? . . . I command ye, therefore, upon the Peril of your Lives, to depart immediately out of this Place . . . Ye Venal Slaves, begone! So take away that shining Bauble there, and lock up the Doors."

The "shining bauble" Cromwell referred to was the Mace, which was never seen again. That which the House now uses is therefore a "new" one, dating from 1660.

There followed various Parliaments of Cromwell's own choosing, punctuated by periods when he governed without it and stabled his horses in the Palace crypt to show his contempt. But England soon tired of dictatorship, and soon after his death Parliament had no hesitation in offering the crown to Charles, whose father it had beheaded twelve years earlier. But the Commons kept a tight hold of his purse-strings.

It is from the reign of Charles II that the Cabinet system of government originated, beginning as a small committee of the Privy Council. Charles trusted few of his fifty-odd Councillors, with the result that an inner Council of five developed. It was known as the Cabal from the first letters of the names of its five members (and is therefore the forebear of such familiar diminutives as Pluto, Shaef, and Uno).

The comparative confidence engendered by Charles II's reign was largely dissipated when his brother, James II, 1685-1688, succeeded him. So the Commons drew up yet one more historic Declaration of Rights to which the prospective sovereigns, William and Mary, had to listen before the formal offer of the crown was made to them. The Declaration became the Bill of Rights, upon which the constitution of Britain has ever since been based.

The turn of the century found the House of Commons safely emerged from the troubles of the revolutionary period and well set upon its career

OLIVER CROMWELL DISMISSING THE LONG PARLIAMENT, APRIL 20TH, 1653
Contemporary Dutch engraving

of constitutional progress. From now on the House met at regular intervals and with none of the hazards hitherto attendant upon membership—to be increased to 558 in 1707 after the Union with Scotland, and to 658 in 1801 after that with Ireland.

At this time it used to sit at 8 a.m. and usually adjourned by midday. If refreshment was required it could be obtained at any of the numerous taverns and coffee-houses which then clustered round the old Palace. Not until the middle of the eighteenth century did the House sit till after dark, when the number of foot-pads that infested the surrounds of Westminster caused Members to assemble at the call of "Who Goes Home ?" and move off in a body preceded by link-boys with torches.

The ghost of a Member of Stuart or early Georgian times looking down upon a present-day sitting of the Commons would have little difficulty in following the proceedings, which indeed are only superficially different from those of two centuries ago. Even the formal black clothes that have been the fashion for legislators since early in Victoria's reign would not look strange to one who sat with Cromwell's Puritans, though others would miss the rich velvets, the lace jabots and periwigs, the sparkling orders and decorations of a later, more colourful age. Only Mr. Speaker, in full-bottomed wig and black silk gown above his court dress, and the three be-wigged Clerks at the Table who sit at his feet, have not changed their dress with the passing fashions.

The eighteenth century was noteworthy for the growth of the party system, though Macaulay gives 1679 as the year in which the nicknames Whig and Tory were first used. The character of the House developed greatly under Sir Robert Walpole, the first Prime Minister in the modern sense and for twenty-one uninterrupted years (1721-42)—a record that has never since been broken. The emergence of the office of Prime Minister was in part due to the fact that neither of the first two Georges could speak English sufficiently well to be able to take the chair at Cabinet meetings. Strathearn Gordon reminds us that, in contradistinction to the American Constitution, which runs to sixteen pages and can be bought anywhere in the United States, no such document as the British Constitution exists. This being so it is perhaps less surprising that, though the office of Prime Minister has been in existence since 1721, it was not recognised by legislation until the Chequers Estate Act of 1917 endowed it with a country house. Since nobody in Britain ever sat down to write out a Constitution, we have no parallel to Section I (1) of Article II : "The executive power shall be vested in a President of the United States. He shall hold his office during the term of four years, etc."

Walpole's Whig Ministry was the first drawn exclusively from one party, just as he was the first political leader to recognise that no administration is possible without a party majority in the Commons, which in turn can only be maintained by partisan activity in the constituencies. And by his resignation in 1742, after an adverse vote, was established the important principle that a Prime Minister who has lost the support of the House can no longer hold office.

His place, after the intervention of one or two mediocrities, was filled by William Pitt—the "terrible Cornet of Horse" whom Walpole had deprived of his commission some years earlier in an attempt to suppress him. It was an age of giants. Even to-day the speeches of Burke, Fox, Sheridan, North and the two Pitts make excellent reading. St. Stephen's Hall continuously resounded to oratory distinguished by grace and scholarship such as cannot be sustained in times when M.P.s get no leisure. An age, also, that was unique in opportunity. Or how else could Pitt the Younger have become Chancellor of the Exchequer in 1782 at the age of twenty-three, and Prime Minister a year later ? (The last three Premiers—Chamberlain, Churchill and Attlee—became so at 67, 66 and 62 respectively, and not since Lord Rosebery became Prime Minister in 1894 at the age of 47 has there been one under fifty.)

Just as the first part of the century was dominated by Walpole, so was the last by Pitt the Younger and Fox, whose personal rivalries and gladia-

The House of Commons in the Eighteenth Century
Speaker Onslow in the Chair, the Prime Minister, Sir Robert Walpole, standing at his side
Engraving after William Hogarth and Sir James Thornhill, 1730

torial contests were only subsequently matched by those of Disraeli and Gladstone. Pitt and Fox face each other still, in marble statuary, and, appropriately, in St. Stephen's Hall which was for so long the scene of their triumphs. One may hope that the scores of patient visitors, who now daily sit for hours in that Hall while awaiting a place in the gallery, know their history books, though indeed the cold stone slabs on which their personal queues rest can hardly be conducive to interesting retrospection.

The last years in St. Stephen's are memorable for the stormy debates which took place over the reform of Parliamentary representation, which was so unsatisfactory that by 1830 public indignation could no longer be ignored. At this time some two hundred and fifty constituencies—the rotten boroughs—were controlled by the aristocracy. Many were customarily sold to the highest bidder, the average price for a seat then being about £6,000. In some cases these boroughs did not even exist. For example Old Sarum was but a stretch of grazing land, the seven non-resident voters having to pitch a tent whenever it was necessary to elect their two Members. At the same time the new manufacturing towns were still unrepresented. Thus Manchester (133,000), Birmingham (85,000) and Leeds (83,000) returned no Members to Parliament, while Cornwall elected thirty-six. The new Bill abolished the rotten boroughs and re-allocated parliamentary seats to correspond more nearly to the distribution of the population. It also increased the franchise, but as this was fixed on a property basis five men out of six were still without a vote, and it was not until the Acts of 1867 and 1884 that the artisan and labouring classes were admitted. The Reform Bill, after much controversy, was passed in 1832. But the new order of Commons men were not to sit long in St. Stephen's, for the great fire of 1834 was soon to destroy almost the whole of the rambling Old Palace except Westminster Hall. That this historic building did not perish also was due to the exertions of Lord Melbourne, Prime Minister and young Victoria's mentor, who took personal command of the firemen and soldiery when all seemed lost.

The Select Committees appointed by both Houses in 1835 recommended that the Houses of Parliament be rebuilt in the style of the Gothic Revival, being under the misapprehension that this popular vogue was a national, English style. From ninety-seven entries in an open competition was selected the design of thirty-nine-year-old Charles Barry, a comparatively unknown man who thus overnight became the most famous architect of his day. So he it was who is principally responsible for this great, greyish limestone mass with all its towers and turrets, its eleven hundred rooms, its hundred staircases and two miles of passages. Most of the elaborate embellishments and rich interior detail are the work of his chief assistant, Pugin. Those were not the days of mechanical excavators and electric drills, so it was eighteen years before the Commons' new Chamber was ready to be occupied. They were not to sit in St. Stephen's again, for Barry had decided to convert its burnt-out shell into a lofty passage-way leading from Westminster Hall to the centre of his new Palace. Four brass rosettes in the stone floor were left to mark the position of the Chair in which Charles I had once had the temerity to seat himself in place of Mr. Speaker Lenthall.

By courtesy of the Trustees of the National Portrait Gallery

WILLIAM PITT, THE YOUNGER, ADDRESSING THE COMMONS

Charles James Fox is seen seated on the Opposition Front Bench. Speaker Addington is in the Chair

Oil painting by K. A. Hickel, 1793

By courtesy of the Lord Great Chamberlain

THE HOUSE OF COMMONS DURING A DEBATE
Lithograph after a painting by Joseph Nash, 1858

The new Chamber was built in the now accepted rectangle. More controversial perhaps was its size, with seating for some four hundred only out of the six hundred elected representatives of the people. For the Commons then, as to-day, preferred a comparatively small, intimate Chamber in which no one need raise his voice. Though eighty or ninety per cent of the Members are frequently in the Palace at the same time, it is only once or twice a year that all wish to be in the Chamber together, when those who cannot find room on the benches sit on the floor of the gangways or stand beyond the bar.

The Commons were to sit on the dark green leather seats of this dark-panelled Chamber for eighty-nine years, until, in the blitz of 1941, a bomb entirely destroyed it. They now meet temporarily in the crimson-upholstered and richly gilded Chamber of the Lords, who have fitted up the King's Robing Room for their own purposes. Meanwhile the Commons' own Chamber is being re-built on its former site.

Twelve months after they had moved into Barry's new Chamber, Gladstone introduced his budget of 1853, with income tax at sevenpence. During the next ten years, while Palmerston and Derby held the premierships, the clashing rivalry between Disraeli and Gladstone was already formulating. Though for twenty years Tory and Whig had given place to Conservative and Liberal, it was only when these two men came to lead them that the rival parties began to develop their special characteristics—advocacy of imperial greatness and internal reform respectively. And it was under the guidance of these two great statesmen, who were to dominate the Commons and English political life for nearly forty years, that the House of Commons gave structure to many of the domestic reforms of to-day. Thus the Conservatives legalised the position of Trades Unions, introduced the first factory and mines legislation and established the principle of free education and municipal housing, while to the credit of the Liberal Party stand compulsory education, the secret ballot, railway legislation, cheap newsprint and other important measures.

To the reforms of the twentieth century, Labour M.P.s were able to contribute. The first, Keir Hardie, was elected for West Ham in 1892, but for some time the growth of the Party was slow. It was not until 1922, when they were returned with 142 Members, that they were strong enough to form the Opposition. But in 1910 they numbered forty and, with the Irish Nationalists, held the decisive position, since, at the Election of that year, the Liberal ministerialists had won only two more seats than the Conservative Opposition. The price for keeping the Government in office was to be Home Rule for Ireland and labour legislation, but before either could be undertaken it was necessary to deal with the power of veto of the House of Lords.

Until 1908 the relationship between the Lords and the Commons had, on the whole, been cordial and co-operative, though there were short

MR. SPEAKER GULLY READING A MESSAGE FROM THE CROWN
ON THE ACCESSION OF EDWARD VII
Pen and wash drawing by J. Walter Wilson for the *Illustrated London News*, January 30th, 1901

periods of violent disagreement. (To avoid provocation both Houses habitually refer to each other's proceedings as occurring in "another place.") But so long as the House of Lords possessed the constitutional power to veto any measure sponsored by the people's elected representatives, it was inevitable that a serious constitutional crisis would arise sooner or later. When, therefore, in 1909, the Lords rejected the Government's Finance Bill, and in doing so negatived its annual budget, the General Election of 1910, with the Lords' power of veto as the issue, was inevitable.

The newly-elected House of Commons passed the Parliament Bill, the effect of which was to reduce the power of the House of Lords to delaying legislation only. The Lords rejected it. Asquith at once went to the country, and another General Election showed that public opinion was unchanged. In the face of this decision of the constituencies, and threatened with the creation of four hundred new Radical peers, the House of Lords had no option but to accept the Parliament Bill. By this measure any Money Bill—so certified by the Speaker—was to receive the Royal Assent within one month of being sent to the Lords by the Commons, and any other Bill if passed by the Commons in three successive sessions. So ended the great constitutional crisis of 1909-11, and so rests the matter to this day.

The Asquith Government now had to pay its debt to the Irish and Labour men, without whose votes the Parliament Act would not have got through the Commons. There followed various measures of social legislation, and the payment of a salary of £400 a year to Members, a dispensation long sought by Labour M.P.s. The Home Rule Bill made slow progress, confronted as the Government was by the prospect of civil war in Ulster. Before it reached its final stage, German columns were advancing into Belgium, and the controversy was postponed until after the war.

In 1916 the Liberal Ministry was replaced by a Coalition whose leader, Lloyd George, introduced the Representation of the People Act of 1918 which added thirteen millions to the electorate, including women for the first time. In the following year Viscountess Astor was elected for the Sutton Division of Plymouth, and the first woman M.P. took her seat in Parliament. But though that is more than twenty years ago, and though women have done excellent work, they have never yet exceeded three and a half per cent of the total membership.

Between 1914 and 1918 the flower of the nation perished upon the battlefield. Whether due to this, or to some more obscure cause, the House of Commons proved singularly barren in statesmanship during the twenty years which followed. Conservative administrations found no solution for unemployment, not even in the manufacture of the armaments which were so soon to be so urgently required. Meanwhile the Parliamentary Labour Party, though nourished on slogans such as "Arms for Spain" (or China or Abyssinia) was still so pacifist as to oppose not only the conscription of Britons, but frequently also voluntary recruiting.

The Englishman's sense of frustration and impotence, while Hitler swooped from coup to coup, was such that, at any rate in the Commons, the war was entered upon with almost a sense of deliverance. The mood of the House, said Mr. Greenwood, speaking for the Opposition on September 3rd, 1939, was now "one of relief and one of composure and one of resolution." In that spirit Members listened to speeches on the declaration of war, and then proceeded to pass four formal resolutions for the financing of Bills before settling down to work on the Committee Stage of the National Service (Armed Forces) Bill.

So continued the regular flow of legislation—the Agricultural Wages (Regulation) Amendment Bill, the Colonial Development Bill and so forth —with only now and then a minor storm over the shortcomings of the Ministry of Supply or Information. But the sense of relief at the declaration of war had soon been replaced by the more familiar one of anxiety and frustration, which was to find its outlet in the historic Debate upon the conduct of the Norwegian Campaign, which took place on May 7th and

8th, 1940. The judgment delivered at the conclusion of it, as expressed by the votes cast, was surely the most momentous of any in the long history of the House of Commons.

The Prime Minister, Neville Chamberlain, opened the Debate and made as good a case as could ever be made out for defeat. But the high tide of his power and influence began to set when L. S. Amery rose to speak four hours later. He quoted from a speech made by Cromwell three hundred years before, when the dash of Prince Rupert's cavalry was beating the Commons' troops, just as that of Hitler's plotters and pilots had now driven their successors out of Norway—"Your troops are most of them old decayed serving-men and tapsters and such kind of fellows . . . you must get men of a spirit that are likely to go as far as they will go, or you will be beaten still." Mr. Amery concluded his speech with the words of Cromwell to the Long Parliament: "Depart, I say, and let us have done with you. In the name of God, go!"

When the vote was taken, thirty-three Conservatives went into the Lobby with the Opposition and many more abstained. As the tellers stood before Mr. Speaker and announced the division figures, which revealed that the Government majority had fallen to eighty, a roar of cheers broke out and the cry: "Resign!" The Prime Minister, gaunt and pale, rose and walked out of the House alone to decide upon his course of action.

His place was taken, as all the world knows, by Winston Churchill. The new Prime Minister's grim greeting to the House was: "I have nothing to offer but blood, toil, tears and sweat." And in the House of Commons, as the struggle developed and the scene darkened, Mr. Churchill made those famous speeches which fired the resolve of all those who were fighting for liberty in the air, on sea or on land, at their furnaces, presses and lathes, or underground in either sense of the word, at home and overseas.

"We shall go on to the end. We shall fight in France. We shall fight on the seas and oceans. We shall fight with growing confidence and growing strength in the air. We shall defend our island, whatever the cost may be. We shall fight on the beaches, we shall fight on the landing grounds, we shall fight in the fields and in the streets, we shall fight in the hills. We shall never surrender."

Thus spoke Mr. Churchill in 1940, his notes resting upon the despatch box deeply scarred by Gladstone's signet ring. Under his leadership Conservatives, Labour men and Liberals put aside their differences, so that, at the end of hostilities, he was able to say that the House of Commons had "proved itself the strongest foundation for waging war that has ever been seen in the whole of our long history. . . ."

Thus the second Great War drew to its victorious conclusion. On April 24th, 1945, Mr. Speaker stood before his Chair and once again switched on the great light above Big Ben, saying as he did so:

Big Ben at Night

"I pray that, with God's blessing, this light will shine henceforth not only as an outward and visible sign that the Parliament of a free people is assembled in free debate, but also that it may shine as a beacon of sure hope in a sadly torn and distracted world."

THOSE noble words were spoken by Colonel the Rt. Hon. Douglas Clifton Brown M.P., 139th in succession since Sir Thomas Hungerford was elected in 1377 to have "les paroles pour les Communes." He was to speak for the House, in particular by representing the views of the Commons to the King. This is the origin of the somewhat anomalous name for the one Member of the House who is not free to speak.

To-day the office is one to which any ambitious Member might well aspire, but in earlier times when the Speaker frequently incurred the hostility of a vindictive monarch, it was far from popular. In fact a timid Speaker once had to be held down in the Chair while resolutions which would incur the King's displeasure were passed. We are reminded of this in the customary display of reluctance with which the Speaker-Elect allows himself to be dragged to the Chair by his sponsors.

On special occasions, principally in connection with the Crown, the Speaker still exercises his historic function of representing the Commons and acting as their spokesman. But his main duty is nowadays to preside over the sittings of the House and regulate its proceedings according to its customs and Standing Orders, upon the interpretation of which he is the supreme authority.

It must be obvious that this is no easy task, particularly when, as frequently happens, personal and party feelings run high. It calls for the exercise of tact, understanding and good humour, combined with firmness and, above all, scrupulous impartiality. As a former Speaker, Lord Ullswater, observed, the office does not require brilliant or rare qualities, so much as common qualities in a rare degree. One might add presence of mind to the list of indispensable qualifications. For the Speaker must be able to name a Member without an instant's hesitation—some Speakers are said to have made a practice of studying Members' faces with a photograph album and a pair of field-glasses, from a window overlooking the Terrace!

And at any moment Mr. Speaker may be confronted with an entirely novel situation. For example, in 1930 a Member seized the Mace. A few years later another retaliated to the interjection "Go back to Poland!" by crossing the floor and boxing the offender's ears. And in 1944 the newly-elected Scottish Nationalist M.P. sought to take his seat without the customary sponsors.

It is seldom that the Speaker has to use his wide powers to deal with disorder. It is usually sufficient for him to stand up, upon which every other Member must sit down, and make a few well-chosen observations. But if a Member persists in being disorderly the Speaker can direct him to "resume his seat" or to leave the Chamber. In the last resort he can order the arrest of a Member and his confinement in the Tower of Big Ben,

Staircase in the Speaker's House

though not since Mr. Bradlaugh was so dealt with in 1880 (for taking his seat after refusing to take the oath) has this been necessary.

It is, of course, the respect with which the Speaker, both in his office and his person is held, rather than the disciplinary powers in reserve, which is responsible for his success. Though the Speakership goes traditionally to a Member from the largest party, ministerialists would only nominate a Member acceptable to the House as a whole. And since the choice rests with the whole House, no Minister acts as proposer or seconder. A contest for the Speakership is possible. The last time this happened was in 1895, when Mr. Speaker Gully was elected by eleven votes.

In practice the Speaker remains in office irrespective of changes of Government. In this tradition the Labour majority of 1945 re-elected the Conservative Member who was appointed Speaker in 1943. Since at a General Election he stands before his constituents as "the Speaker seeking re-election," and not as the nominee of a political party, it has not been customary to oppose him, though an exception has been made to this at the last two Elections.

At his re-election as Speaker in 1945, Colonel Clifton Brown said: "I have been a back-bencher for a long time, and when we saw the two Front Benches, Government and Opposition, putting their heads together, we always used to say: 'Well, the back-bencher is going to get a dirty deal.' As Speaker I am not the Government's man, nor the Opposition's man. I am the House of Commons' man and, I believe, above all the back-bencher's man."

To protect the House against the powers and encroachments of the executive, and to protect minorities within the House itself and safeguard their rights, is one of the most important of the Speaker's functions. For, as W. J. Brown has said: "The humblest back-bencher is no less than a Member, and the greatest Minister is no more than a Member, in respect of his Parliamentary rights."

Speaker Lowther in 1919 observed that he had already sat through 35,840 speeches in the House.

No Speaker could remain in the Chair all the time and preserve his sanity. So there is a Deputy who presides when Mr. Speaker leaves the Chair for refreshment and occasionally to rest.

The Speaker's office carries a salary of £5,000 a year, and he has a house within the Palace. On retirement he is offered a viscounty and receives a pension of £4,000. He is the only subject who holds levées, at which court dress is worn.

On ceremonial occasions the Speaker rides in his State Coach, escorted by one trooper of the Household Cavalry; the coach weighs 2¾ tons and, since a hundred years ago, it has always been drawn by the dray-horses of Messrs. Whitbread, the firm in which a Speaker of that time was a partner.

The Prime Minister takes precedence before the Speaker, as seventh and ninth subjects in the land respectively. But the Prime Minister has no special rights or privileges in the House, which indeed he can only address when called upon to do so by the Speaker.

By courtesy of the Lord Great Chamberlain

CHARLES I AND SPEAKER LENTHALL

Fresco in the Houses of Parliament, by C. West Cope, Jr., c. 1850

By courtesy of the Lord Great Chamberlain

THE SPEAKER'S PROCESSION, 1884

The Speaker is Sir H. B. W. Brand. The Prime Minister, W. E. Gladstone, is seen standing on the right

Oil painting by F. W. Lawson

THE COMMONS AT WORK

IT is now time to describe the place and function of the House of Commons within the Constitution ; or, in other words, what it *does* and how it works.

The Commons are so much the dominant partner of the two Houses that they are now often inaccurately referred to as "Parliament." So we call a Member of the House of Commons a "Member of Parliament," though a peer who has taken his seat in the Lords is no less a Member of Parliament just because it occurs to nobody to put "M.P." after his name. Used correctly "Parliament" means the Sovereign, the Lords and the Commons who, acting together, form the legislature.

Since the Parliament Act of 1911 the House of Lords have been little more than a revising body. But in this respect their work is valuable. For example they returned the Coal Industry Nationalisation Bill (1946) with no less than fifteen pages of Amendments, all of which were accepted by the Minister in charge of the Bill in the Commons. And the debates in the Lords are generally considered to reach a higher standard than those of the Commons.

The part played by the Crown has been well described by Gordon : "By virtue of his central position and continuous office, the King has still enormous potential influence through the discussions which proceed incessantly between himself and the leading figures of the nation. He is perpetually in touch with the Government. . . . Whatever crises may arise have first to be brought before the Sovereign." Walter Bagehot has said that the King has three rights : the right to be consulted, the right to encourage, the right to warn. He adds that a sensible monarch would want no others. Constitutionally the King has two important functions. The first is to appoint the Prime Minister, though in practice his choice is invariably the leader or leader-designate of the party that has the majority in the Commons. The second is to dissolve Parliament. In this the King is guided by the advice of the Prime Minister, though in exceptional circumstances, and with an alternative Prime Minister at hand who would command a Commons majority, he could with propriety act contrary to his official advice.

There are normally three occasions on which the Prime Minister will ask the King for a Dissolution. Firstly, if he wishes to introduce important legislation of a controversial nature for which his party received no mandate at the previous General Election. Baldwin acted in this way when he wished to introduce tariffs in 1923. Secondly, if the Government is defeated by a vote on an issue which is tantamount to one of confidence. And, thirdly, when the Government considers it to be an auspicious moment towards the end of its normal five-year term ; for, except in wartime, no Parliament can last for longer than five years. The sequel to a Dissolution is, of course, an immediate General Election, voting taking place on the seventeenth day.

Broadly speaking, any British subject over the age of twenty-one, of either sex, is eligible for election provided he or she can produce a deposit of £150, which is returned if the candidate secures one-eighth of the total number of votes polled. But there is a small category of excepted persons which includes peers (other than those of the Irish peerage), judges, clergymen, felons, bankrupts and lunatics—if only those who have been certified. Some of those who stand for Parliament do so as Independents; at the General Election of 1945, the 1,683 candidates for 640 seats included 75 Independents, of whom 14 were elected. The majority—90.2% in 1945—are the nominees of the three principal political parties. Independence is often a characteristic of University Members, seven of the twelve elected in 1945 having no party affiliations.

The party which has won the largest number of seats is entitled to form the Government, and as soon as the Election results are known the King commissions its leader to do so. The latter consults his senior colleagues and then invites those whom he has chosen to accept the principal offices: the Exchequer, Foreign Office, Board of Trade, the Dominions and Colonial Offices, the Service ministries and so forth. A few posts are allotted to peers, in order that the Government shall be represented in both Houses. The party leader then informs the King that he is in a position to form a Government, and is himself sworn in as Prime Minister.

After a short interval, during which the senior Ministers in the Cabinet decide upon the Government's legislative programme and the junior Ministers outside the Cabinet are appointed, Parliament is summoned for its formal opening by the King. This is an impressive ceremony, particularly in normal times when full dress uniform and the peers' scarlet and ermine robes are worn. The King and Queen seat themselves on the two thrones which always stand behind the Woolsack in the House of Lords, one of which vain Victoria had raised an inch or two so that she would not sit lower than her taller Consort. The King then says: "My Lords, pray be seated." All do so except Mr. Speaker and the Members of the Commons who are standing beyond the bar at the far end of the Chamber. The King then proceeds to read the "King's Speech," which in fact is that of his Prime Minister, since it outlines the Government's programme for the next session, *i.e.* parliamentary year. Thus, after a preamble: "It will be the purpose of my Government to . . . Legislation will be submitted to you for . . . My Ministers will press on with . . . You will be asked to approve . . ." The King concludes with: "I pray that Almighty God may give His blessing to your counsels."

The Speaker and the Commons return to their own Chamber and there begins a debate upon the Government's proposals which lasts for at least a week. It takes the form of a Motion "That an humble Address of Thanks

The Prime Minister, The Rt. Hon. Clement Attlee, in his Room in the House, March 1947

be presented to His Majesty for His Majesty's Most Gracious Speech," to which Members who wish to express disapproval of the Government's programme will, by means of an Amendment, endeavour to tack on ". . . but regrets that the Gracious Speech contains no reference to . . ." or "gives no assurance of . . ." The Amendments, if pressed to a vote, will be defeated in the division lobbies, since the supporters of the Government are in the majority. At the end of the allotted number of days the Speaker puts the Motion to the House with the usual formula "Those that are of this opinion say : 'Aye.' To the contrary ?" This is followed by : "The Ayes have it," unless his "To the contrary ?" was answered by cries of "No !" In that case he will call out "Clear the lobbies !" This classic phrase announces that a division is to take place. Members file down the Chamber in a body and divide beyond the bar, some turning to the right to enter the "Aye" lobby and others to the left for the "No" lobby, their names and number being duly recorded as they pass through. At the same time the division bells ring all over the Palace, and the libraries, restaurants and committee rooms all contribute their quota of Members who come hurrying forward to strike another blow for freedom or reaction—according to your point of view.

When the Motion "That an humble Address of Thanks, etc." is passed, the new Government has been formally accepted by the House. But from now on it has to descend from such broad generalities as "a measure for the reorganisation of . . ." to the pernickety details of the actual Bills.

The activities of the House of Commons fall broadly under three headings : legislation, finance and criticism. While a Government can make certain administrative changes under powers conferred by previous Acts, any major reorganisation, and frequently also very simple matters, will require both new laws and the repeal of, or alteration to, the law already in existence. This is "legislation"—something which only Parliament can do. It means a new Act of Parliament, and let us consider how one comes into being.

We will assume that the Government decides to reorganise the national system of education. The first step is for the Minister to tell his senior civil servants at the Ministry of Education the broad outline of the scheme he has in mind. Together they will work out the details of it. Meanwhile he has consultations with the principal interests involved—in this case local authorities and their education officers, religious bodies concerning their own schools, the Ministry of Health in regard to school meals and medical inspections, representatives of parents' and teachers' organisations, and so on. With their assistance the scheme is perfected, at least in the eyes of the Minister. The legal requirements are then set down in the form of a Bill, by highly-skilled parliamentary draftsmen. Now it is ready for Parliament, but it may be some time before it can be introduced, as other Ministers are also anxious to bring forward their own pet projects.

The Bill enters the House with what is called its "First Reading," though this is no more than a formality. It means in effect that "Education Bill" appears on the Order Paper, which gives notice to Members that copies of it are now available for them to read. A few weeks later comes the

THE SERJEANT-AT-ARMS CARRYING THE MACE

"Second Reading," and on this occasion the principles, but not the details, of the Bill are debated. But during the Committee Stage, which follows next, the Bill is gone through clause by clause, line by line and word by word. Originally this usually took place in the Chamber before the whole House, but owing to pressure of business most Bills now pass this scrutiny before smaller Committees sitting upstairs. Many amendments are debated and some of them accepted by the Minister, to the great improvement of the Bill. In a long and complicated measure this stage may last for weeks.

At the Report Stage the Bill, as amended "in Committee," is reported back to the House and further amendments may be proposed. Then follows the "Third Reading" debate, on the Bill, as it has finally emerged from the scrutiny of the House, and this is the last discussion upon the measure before it is sent up to "another place"—endorsed in ancient Norman French "*soit baillé aux Seigneurs*." When it has been passed there it goes to the King for the Royal Assent, after which it becomes an "Act."

But it should not be assumed that these successive stages—Second Reading, Committee Stage, Report Stage and Third Reading—follow swiftly upon each other. For they have to be fitted in, not only with other Bills but also with the House's second function—its financial work. This is considerable, for one of the principal duties of the Commons is to approve both the raising of revenue and the way that it is spent. So the Chancellor annually brings forward his Budget, which sets out his proposals for taxation, and many are the days (and nights) which the House spends discussing them. Only the Government can initiate proposals for taxation and expenditure, and these must first be discussed in Committee as well as later by the House itself, a precaution against hasty decisions. Every year, also, the House has to pass the Estimates, which are statements of expenditure estimated by the various Government Departments to be necessary for the ensuing year. And since the House is entitled to insist upon "the redress of grievances" before voting supplies to the Crown, Members have the right to criticise the Minister's department and give him advice before concurring with his Estimate, a right of which they always avail themselves.

In that respect the financial work of the House is part of its third function—the critical. To discuss and question continuously both the policy and the administration of the Government is surely as important as anything it does. So, in addition to debates upon supply and current legislation, special opportunities for criticism are provided. Question-time is useful for showing up shortcomings, not only in a Minister's policy but also in his personal ability. So are the Debates upon the Adjournment—the last half-hour of each day's business which, together with the last day before the House adjourns for a recess, is allotted to back-benchers for discussing any matter of administration. Many and varied are these, as can be seen from the following subjects raised during the current week at the time of writing: The British Commonwealth, Official Forms, Cattle breeding, Restaurant Prices, Industries in Staffordshire, Atomic Energy Commission, Army Recruiting.

In addition to these daily facilities for criticism and advice, debates frequently take place upon current affairs. Formerly one day in each of certain weeks was set aside for Private Members' Motions, *e.g.* "that in the opinion of this House bread rationing is obnoxious, injurious and unnecessary, and ought to be abolished." This was in addition to certain other days reserved for Private Members' Bills, on which back-benchers could introduce new legislation. But since the beginning of the late war the executive have taken over the whole of Private Members' time for Government business, a development which many people consider to be disquieting.

THE CLERKS OF THE COMMONS

Theoretically, at any time while engaged in any of its different functions, whether for example on current legislation, a motion of policy or a supply Estimate, the Government can be defeated in the division lobbies. And as this so very rarely happens, since Government supporters are in the majority, the reader may well wonder what is the point of an Opposition which is able to express its views but remains impotent when it comes to enforcing them, and whether there is much point in the party system at all.

W. J. Brown, Independent M.P. for Rugby, has written:

"Any gathering will automatically divide itself into two parts. The men and women will be either of the Conservative or the Radical type of mind. The Conservative mind, at its best, possesses a strong historical sense, values the legacy from our forefathers, and is reluctant to gamble too highly with a not intolerable present for the sake of a hypothetical better future. The Radical type of mind is so conscious of injustices, so confident that society could be made very much better, that it is prepared to incur considerable risks in making changes."

That this fundamental division of outlook and approach exists is undeniably true, and it is responsible for the broad classification of political thought into "Right" and "Left." Equally it draws the dividing line between parties in the Commons. Moreover the party system is highly convenient, for teamwork is necessary both among Ministers administering the Government and for their support in the House. Only good teamwork will make certain that there is always the majority necessary to ensure the Government's safe passage. Meanwhile, though the Opposition may be beaten in the division lobbies, it acts as a ginger group and scrutineer, makes its voice heard and mobilises public opinion against despotic or irresponsible action on the part of the executive.

The day-to-day necessity of mustering sufficient platoons of Members to maintain the Government's majority (or the Opposition's solidarity) is responsible for the Whip, originally a written summons and now also the name for those Members who are responsible for thus marshalling their parties.

Many writers have called attention to the danger to parliamentary democracy that is inherent in the powers of the Whips used in conjunction with the party machines. These are twofold : to punish and to reward. An M.P. who persistently votes and speaks against his party will, after due warning, have the party Whip withdrawn from him. This is equivalent to expulsion and means that pressure from party headquarters will be brought to bear in the rebel's constituency, seeking to ensure that he is not re-elected. The rewards disposed of by the Whips are in the nature of promotion or patronage, and one of the official names of the Government Chief Whip is the "Patronage Secretary." The Whips naturally prefer a yes-man to a no-man or a not-always man, so it is the "safe party man who can be relied upon" who receives the Chief Whip's often decisive recommendation, whether it be for an under-secretaryship, a colonial governorship, a knighthood or peerage in the Honours List, or even a free trip abroad as part of a parliamentary delegation.

The danger is a real one, and the balance perhaps tilted in favour of the executive and the party machine. But in the House of Commons there are men of independent judgment and the courage to express it, as many a headstrong Minister has found to his cost. Though the Government is rarely defeated in a division, it frequently has the wisdom to give way. Some of these occasions, such as the repudiation of the Hoare-Laval pact, receive widespread publicity, while others, for example the abandonment of the proposed purchase tax on books, attract little notice. Even a single

The Libraries : The Silence Room
The engraved panels record the names of past Speakers

Member, if his case be a strong one, can compel the Government to act, as is shown by the record of some of the comparatively few Independent M.P.s. Miss Rathbone successfully advocated the necessity for children's allowances, A. P. Herbert for divorce reform, and W. D. Kendall for an increase in servicemen's pay. W. J. Brown, the champion of state pensioners and unestablished civil servants, has also emerged triumphant from several battles with the executive.

So we see that it is Members of Parliament—some sixty in number—who are put in charge of the great departments of State. These are the men who individually, but in accordance with a collective Cabinet plan, govern the country. And it is to the remaining 580 M.P.s collectively that they must report their proposals and progress, and whose critical scrutiny they must pass before they will receive the funds without which they cannot carry on government.

OUR MEMBERS

WHAT sort of men are these Members of Parliament, who legislate for every stage of our lives ?—who decide that we must be educated, the conditions under which we work, what shall happen to us if we become unemployed, or ill, or destitute, or break the law, what taxes and insurance we pay and what we get for it, how much we shall eat, and many other intimate, personal matters? What exactly are their qualifications ? Do they earn what we pay them ? What sort of lives do they live?

First of all our legislators are a cross-section of the nation. As a wit once remarked, the House of Commons is like the zoo for it contains "one of everything": industrialists, trades union officials, farmers, doctors, journalists, manual workers, men of independent means, shopkeepers, barristers, a sailor or two, schoolmasters, engine drivers, tailors, stockbrokers, housewives ; there is even a professional juggler. But though most occupations are included, they are by no means proportionately represented. For example, in the last two Parliaments every other M.P. has been in one of three categories : a company director, a trades union official or a lawyer. This over-representation of the "talking classes" is due to the fact that few M.P.s can afford to live on their salary and these three occupations are those which can most easily be combined with a parliamentary career.

The Member's salary was raised to £600 in 1937 and to £1,000 in 1946. Out of this he has to pay all expenses except his railway fare to London, the main items being secretarial assistance, postage, travelling about his constituency and the extra cost of living in two places. So for the sake of economy most M.P.s share a secretary, though they would be more efficient with one each—(compare an American Congressman drawing £2,000 a year for "clerk-hire"). The expenses can be deducted from the salary before income tax is paid on the remainder of it. Even so, a Member who lives in his constituency as well as in London can hardly spend less than about £700 on necessary expenses. In consequence nearly every M.P. has an additional source of income. Many, in all parties, possess private means. Others receive a supplement from an organisation such as a trades union or employers' association, the danger of which, whether real or imaginary, is considered to be the temptation to promote purely sectional interests. The remainder, perhaps the majority, have to neglect the nation's affairs while dissipating much of their time and energy upon the day-to-day business of earning a living. It is to be hoped that Members will one day have the courage to put this right by voting themselves an adequate expenses allowance. There is one other financial reform which is long overdue. Parliament is responsible for 500 million human beings in India and the Colonial Empire, but few Members can ever afford to visit our overseas possessions. Every M.P. should be entitled to one air passage a year, to any part of the British Empire.

THE CENTRAL HALL

What are the qualities required to make a good Member ? I would put sympathy first, for without it we cannot hope to understand the aspirations, the problems and frustrations of those whose lot we seek to improve. Strength of character, energy, ability and sound judgment are necessary, in order to find the right answers to some at least of the perplexing problems with which we are confronted. Also invaluable is an intimate knowledge of one or more activities of the nation, whether it be industry, agriculture, education, local government, or any other upon which a great number of our citizens are engaged.

To these qualifications should be added physical fitness and stamina, for the life of a conscientious Member is arduous in the extreme. This is the opinion of Lord Snell, a former Labour M.P. :

"As a result of seven years' experience, I am convinced that the average Member of Parliament works at greater pressure and for longer hours than nine-tenths of those who elect him, and that if the factory worker, miner or engineer had the same strain put upon him, he would down tools within a month and demand better conditions of work."

While Parliament is sitting, the average day's work is one of twelve hours. For those who are not on a Standing Committee, meeting at 10.30 a.m., and who do not go to business, the morning passes quickly in reading and writing. Correspondence with constituents, and on their behalf with Ministers, Government departments, employers, local officials and so forth, takes up time. An M.P. must above all be well-informed, which entails much perusing of newspapers, government publications, Parliamentary Reports (called *Hansard* after the family which edited and printed them from 1829 to 1889), and a good deal of miscellaneous research. Such is the pressure upon M.P.s to-day that it can be doubted whether more than 25% of them find time to read 25% of the Bills they vote upon. The afternoon and evening is divided between attendance in the Chamber and upon committees, work in the libraries, and meals. It is no uncommon thing for a Member to spend two or three days preparing a speech, followed by two or even three in the Chamber continuously jumping up at the end of other speeches in an endeavour to catch Mr. Speaker's eye, and even then not being called. Many find this a considerable nervous strain. It is seldom that the House adjourns before 10.30 p.m., and often it is much later. In the present Government's first year, 1945-46, the House sat after 11 p.m. for eighty-one hours. Of course there are a few lazy men in Parliament, just as there are in every walk of life; but this is too often the fault of the apathetic electors who sent them there.

At weekends and during recesses a Member has his constituency obligations to fulfil. He must get around and meet his people and listen to their problems. There is much that he can do to help them, especially in these days when many people find themselves confused by regulations. He has about 60,000 electors in his Division. Many of them voted for his opponent and are, even now, plotting for his downfall at the next election. Nevertheless he represents the whole constituency, and in personal matters he will do his best for them too. Very likely he must also make good use of the weekend and recess to make up arrears in earning his living. It is possible that he may also like to have some private life.

The Crypt

It sometimes happens that a Member's votes and speeches find disfavour with the association in his constituency which adopted him and largely secured his election. In that case they will summon a meeting and give him an opportunity for an explanation. But, even if they are still dissatisfied, they cannot call upon him to resign, for a Member of Parliament is a representative and in no sense a delegate. As Burke said to the electors of Bristol in 1774: "Your representative owes you not his industry only, but his judgment; and he betrays, instead of serving you, if he sacrifices it to your opinion."

If an M.P. wishes to resign, he does so by applying for the office of Bailiff of the Chiltern Hundreds or of the Manor of Northstead. Though these posts no longer exist they are still technically offices of profit under the Crown, which has been a disqualification for Membership since the time when monarchs sought to influence the Commons by a too liberal dispensation of preferments and pensions.

That so few resign, except from causes beyond their control, is proof that the fascination of the life far outweighs its disadvantages. In particular Members have the enduring reward of being in a position which is almost unique in its opportunities for helping other people. And all appreciate their good fortune in membership of what used to be called the "best club in London." As the House provides its Members with few of the comforts and amenities of a first-class social club, this expression refers entirely to the companionship. It is probably true to say that no other company contains such a richness and diversity of personalities, without which their owners would neither have sought nor achieved election. Life-long friendships, transcending all political alignments, are born in the stuffy little Members' smoking-room which is fortunately too small to encourage party exclusiveness in relaxation. To this must be added a fine cameraderie with the clerks and officials, lobby correspondents, messengers, policemen and others whose daily work brings them to the Palace. It must be a sad moment for any man (or woman) when, on his last night as a Member, he sees the great light above Big Ben switched off to the immemorial cry of "Who Goes Home ?"

DEMOCRACY AND CITIZENSHIP

A POSTSCRIPT upon Parliament, democracy and citizenship.

Our democratic system of Government confers undoubted and great benefits upon our people, but it also confers responsibility. Apathetic electors who every three or four years put a cross against a name for no other reason than because their neighbour or favourite newspaper has told them to do so, cannot complain if things are subsequently not to their liking. For in a democracy the people get no more than the Government they deserve.

It follows, therefore, that our citizens should, if only in their own interest, take part in the workings of democracy. This they can do in several ways. Firstly by exercising care in the selection of their own representative, whether it be for the House of Commons or the local council. And having elected him they should insist upon a high standard of service. Nor should they shirk from subsequently trying to influence him, either by writing or in an interview. To do this they must, of course, themselves be well-informed on current issues. When possible they should follow parliamentary debates, either through the impartial medium of the B.B.C. or by reading one of the few newspapers which attempt to give a balanced presentation. Occasionally, to study subjects which particularly concern them, they would be well advised to read *Hansard*. It is to be found in

THE CHAMBER OF THE COMMONS, DESTROYED BY A BOMB IN 1941

most public libraries and is obtainable on order from any bookstall (6d. daily, or 1/6 the weekly bound copy). These reports are usually of interest, and often of considerable entertainment, to anybody who has visited the House and listened to a debate and is thus able to picture the proceedings. For those who are in London the House is open to visitors from 10 a.m. to 3.30 p.m. every Saturday, and on all weekdays while the House is in recess. A Member will always be willing to show round a party of his constituents in the mornings, just as he will endeavour to supply special passes to obviate queueing for the public gallery, though at present requests for these far exceed the supply. A visit to the House of Commons greatly stimulates one's interest in parliamentary democracy.

Abraham Lincoln left us many wise sayings. One of them was: "No man is good enough to govern another man without that other's consent," and no truer words have ever been spoken. But they hardly go far enough. Consider his famous definition of democracy: "Government of the people, by the people, for the people." Under any régime there will be government *of* the people. Under our own system of parliamentary democracy there is government *by* the people—some sort of people. But is it necessarily government *for* the people?—that is to say government which, both on a short-term and a long-term basis, is best for the common man?

This will always depend upon the quality of the leaders who emerge from the ranks of our citizens. Equally it depends upon the discrimination of the citizens who choose the leaders by whom, in Lincoln's phrase, they "consent" to be governed. And since judgment can only be sensibly exercised by those who keep themselves informed about government, it behoves us all to take an interest in the doings of Parliament. Otherwise one day it may well come to merit Cromwell's description of the Long Parliament—"intolerably odious to the whole nation." In that event democracy itself will be in danger, and Britain the poorer.

SHORT BIBLIOGRAPHY

The best three short books on Parliament are:

Everybody's Guide to Parliament, 1945, by W. J. Brown M.P. Allen & Unwin.—*Our Parliament*, 1945, by Strathearn Gordon. Hansard Society.—*The Purpose of Parliament*, 1945, by Quintin Hogg M.P. Blandford

Others, to which the Author is also indebted, are:

The History of the Ancient Palace and Late Houses of Parliament at Westminster, 1836, by E. W. Brayley and J. Britton. London.—*Parliament, Past and Present*, (2 vols.) 1902-3, by Arnold Wright and Philip Smith. Hutchinson.—*Parliament*, 1939, by W. I. Jennings. Cambridge University Press.—*Mirror of Britain*, 1941, by J. E. Sewell. Hodder & Stoughton.—*The Speaker of the House of Commons*, 1945, by Phyllis Briers. Hansard Society.—*The Houses of Parliament*, 1945, by Hans Wild and James Pope-Hennessy. Batsford